THE GIFT OF HOW NOT TO BE A CHARITY DICKHEAD THIS CHRISTMAS

BY CHRISTELLE COLLET

ISBN: 9798572856323

DEDICATION

Dedicated to my beautiful and kind Alex, selflessness personified...

CONTENTS

ACKNOWLEDGMENTS

I could not have gifted you this writing without the many amazing people in my life. So special thanks to:

- My editor, Eleanor Shember. Ellie, for your professionalism and generosity. I wanted ruthlessness for perfection's sake, you gave honesty, excellence and compassion while handling this emotional and personal piece.

- Katelyn Ford. Katie, your enthusiasm, and colourful brain has been just what I needed to perfect this book cover.

- Marziya Mohammedali. For authorising the use of their portrait of me in the 'about the author' section. Marziya, your art of photography keeps giving a voice to those who needs to be heard and I am grateful for you.

- My darling husband. Laurent, thank you for allowing me to be raw here and anywhere.

- All my active Facebook friends who engage in our conversations, as uncomfortable as they can be. Thank you for triggering memories that needed to be shared.

- Everyone who has selflessly participated in my happiness with their love and care. I see you.

- Santa for always showing up. Even when I stopped wishing, you kept coming and never gave up until I started wishing back again. You kept my carefree, imaginative, hopeful childhood spirit alive.

.

PREFACE

I am an unashamed Christmas fanatic. Hence why I have been posting about Christmas on social media since 1 November; my excitement, stresses, criticisms, and plannings, all are being shared and discussed.

Something that keeps coming up from conversations around these posts is charity. People will randomly shoehorn into their responses all the charity or charitable thoughts one must have during the holidays. Some would even give detailed descriptions of their charitable actions, with a lot of focus on "teaching kids".

I thus decided to start a different conversation on the topic of financially privileged people, especially parents, making it a point to tell the world about the charitable interests they and their kids have. Also contained within are reflections about socially motivated giving during this time of year.

This memoir is a collection of anecdotes and reflections to serve as a guide for anyone favouring charity this Christmas. While I develop my social media rants further, I invite you to dive in my own life and reflect on the nature of donations, especially during the holidays. Allow my authentic self to give you some pointers on how to do charity without being, well, dickheads.

PROLOGUE

Per Noel, kot to ete?

Father Christmas, where are you?

by Christelle Collet

Per noel, eski to tann mwa?

Father Christmas, do you hear me?

Banla dir mwa to tann tou

They say you hear everything

To trouv tou

You see everything

Me per noel eski to trouv mwa?

But Father Christmas, do you see me?

Parski depi lontan

'Cause it's been a while

To pa vinn kot nou

You haven't been to ours

Monn netoy mo soulier

I cleaned my shoes

Mem li ena trou

Even if they have holes

Enn lastoplas

A band-aid

Inn couver tou

Covered it all

Li bien briye

They're quite shiny

Li bien cocas

They're quite cute

Mank zis to mem

Missing only you

Pou vinn tchek nu

To come see us

Per noel, eski to tann mwa?

Father Christmas, do you hear me?

Banla dir mwa to p pini mwa

They tell me you're punishing me

Kinn arrive?

What *happened?*

Monn fer move?

Was I naughty?

Mo pann fer expre

It was accidental

Mo lame ti tremble

My hand was shaking

Me pa traka

Don't worry

Mami ti la

Mummy was there

Linn couriz mwa

She disciplined me

1, 2, 3 clak

1, 2, 3 slaps

Donk per noel

So Father Christmas

Tonn pardonn mwa?

You forgave me?

Mo promet twa

I promise you

Mo pa pu decevwar twa

I won't disappoint you

1. ADVERTISED CHARITY

"I like to take this time to give to underprivileged people. This is what I am teaching my kids about Christmas."

-        various parents on Facebook.

So wrong!

What is this habit that, whenever Christmas is brought up, my fellow socially-conscious parents have to advertise to the world their charity plans? This phenomenon occurs not only in conversations I start, but all over social media; this continuous circling back to people needing to let others know that they don't *only* partake in the consumerism that is Christmas, they also "give to the poor". The more we progress towards a society that is aware of various injustices, the more the virtue signalling around the holidays increases.

When parents do this advertised charity, it creates at least three distinct feelings.

The first one is that of validation from and to other people who are interacting and love advertising their charity to show that they too are *good* people. This validation will be demonstrated by acclamations or expressed relatability, or encouragement to keep the subject going. I suspect this is the kind of validation that you must seek if you are one who loves advertising charity.

The second distinct feeling that emerges with such a topic is annoyance. Yes, other people are annoyed not to be able to talk about Christmas without some privileged person bringing up charity. They either want to engage in the problematic holiday without guilt *or* they know the issues around Christmas and just want to avoid the obnoxious nature of people who engage in advertised charity. I know that this seems a bit like character assassination. Listen, not every parent guilty of this advertising is a bad person, of course not. But good people can be obnoxious.

The third feeling this whole phenomenon creates is what I relate the most to; advertised charity is quite triggering for people who have experienced, or are experiencing, poverty.

Flashback...

I was placed in an orphanage just after my first birthday. Sure, the orphanage was an attraction park for *charity chasers* (see next chapter), but I was too young to have interesting anecdotes on that topic to share.

When I was five years old, I was placed back to live with my biological mother, her new husband, and their newborn baby. From that time until the age of 11, we lived in extreme poverty in a 'developing country' - Mauritius. We lived in tin shacks that we would build ourselves; we had an outside kitchen and no sanitation. During cyclonic seasons, we would leave our home, go live in shelters until we had built a new shack out of rotting wood logs and rusting tin sheets full of holes. We called our home '*la caz enba la rivier*' (the house by the river).

My mother was employed in a hair salon and her husband as a cleaner at a bank. Before marrying this man and moving there, while I was in the orphanage, my mother was homeless. So, these living conditions were an upgrade in her life. The shack was connected to electricity, which would often get disconnected for arrears, so living with candles became our norm. Living with hazards became our norm.

Sitting outside the beginnings of a rudimentary dry toilet that was never completed.

It was situated by la caz enba la rivier, Mauritius.

I adored Christmas. It was magic for me. Santa, this imaginary being bringing something I really, really wanted. We only had one gift from Santa which I thought was normal. I didn't think about it much because most kids in my school were as poor as me. I only had gifts from my mother thrice a year, for my birthday, Christmas and for New Year. The Christmas holiday brought so much happiness in a very gloomy childhood. I always got what I wanted until the age of 11 when I learnt that Santa wasn't real, thus I stopped my wishing.

I guess my mother saved money and made sure that the one thing I wanted all year would land on my shoes; we did not have Christmas trees, only our shoes under our beds which is the poor-people version of a French tradition. I remember one year I really wanted a violin, I talked about it for months. I would look up at the sky and talk to Santa, begging him for that violin. I did indeed get my plastic toy violin where I pretended to create amazing music. I was happy. When I was ten years old, I asked for a piano. I got my keyboard; now I wonder how many months of savings my mother put in that gift… For the rest of the year, I never asked for anything, nor did I get random gifts. For my birthdays, my mother would give me books and clothes, and each New Year I would get new clothes, as per Mauritian tradition.

Being a poor kid in my poor neighbourhood, I was invited to a lot of charity Christmas events and was recipient of a few charity initiatives. Whether they were organised by the city council, the Church or other charity organisations, I was always present because I wanted presents and cake and fun activities. My childhood memories tell me that they were mostly enjoyable; they formed part of what Christmas magic was for me. They were moments of escapism with people - volunteers - who I mostly never saw again.

As an adult, I now wonder why all that caring happened only during Christmas season. Why did the city council, the Church and other organisations offer me this escapism for only a moment while for the rest of the year I felt alone and forgotten? I think of all the pictures that were taken of me with my friends and the 'other' kids that came with their parents to volunteer, pictures I never saw. I never saw the kids again either, where did they all go? Where did the photos end up and, are they proof that these kids' parents were better people? If there was social media at that time, would my friends and I be referred to in conversations on Facebook that were irrelevant to us as people? Was I a human being that they cared about or was I a prop, a mere actor for poverty porn to be shared with friends to proudly consume?

Now, when I read and hear people during this time advertising their charitable actions, I think of young me and I want to protect her and her dignity. I want to advise her to not go to these events and take these gifts...but then I remember the happiness that it brought her and I feel grateful for the bliss of her ignorance regarding the underlying motivations.

Take note.

So, I ask my fellow adults, is it necessary to expose what you do online, knowing that the poor, and formerly-poor - people like myself - can read your exultations? I am certainly not against giving to people during the holidays, especially to people who need extra love and care. I do challenge the idea of not only waiting for Christmas - and other relevant holidays - to show compassion, and I do challenge the notion that it must be broadcast to the world. Are you after validation of how good a person you are, or do you want to raise issues of inequality and poverty? You certainly can do the latter without giving details of the good you do.

You can start conversations about financial and social inequities. Share articles, unpack your biases. However, be mindful of virtue signalling. Knowing that you will spend any amount of money that will bring your kid's happiness, only to then criticise other people who spend more than you to bring the same happiness to their kids is a bit hypocritical. Constantly bringing up poor people when you are amongst your privileged friends talking about Christmas plans does not prove anything. And when critiquing Christmas gift expenses, perhaps we can step away from the actual 'amount' and consider the idea of consumerism and how it interacts with classism and other marginalisations. Surely, if there was no inequality, no one would care how many gifts one is giving their kids?? Instead, the conversation would focus on the environment instead of actual poverty, which is the argument of choice of those advertising charity.

Yes, Christmas is problematic in many ways and we can and should discuss it. But hopping onto irrelevant Christmas conversations with your main argument describing how good a person you are for the poor is gross. This is very much centring and showing off yourself as a better holiday-er. Even if you get validated by other people with the same gross mindset as you, it makes many of us uncomfortable. A friend of mine shared a meme with me which says:

"When helping the poor, leave the camera at home". I would also add "don't give and tell", and even "don't bring it online".

Perhaps, this Christmas, your gift to the world will be your own reflection and growth? Unless you are a die-hard charity chaser, then you have bigger baggage to unpack.

2 CHARITY CHASERS

Charity Chaser: noun. Plural: charity chasers. Non-gendered.

(Original term)

So wrong!

This term refers to people who chase opportunities to declutter in the name of charity. And when I say decluttering, I am not only talking about trash but also their guilt feelings. Opportunities come as specific profiles: Black and Indigenous women, homeless people, recently single mothers, families with disabled members especially kids, refugee families that just settled in the neighbourhood, orphans, and foster kids.

Charity chasers do not care about the people they're purporting to help, nor what they need. They only desire a place to dump their trash and pretend they are better people because they supposedly helped someone 'needy'.

They will not list the items they are getting rid of on *Buy Sell Swap* pages or exchange and gifting platforms; that would be too much hassle for them, and they would not get the validation they typically seek. Charity shop - also known as op shops - drop-off is not their first choice either; they want to give it to "someone who deserves". For them, someone who deserves is someone who will not be in a position to choose or even refuse. Customers of op shops would have too much agency for the liking of the charity chaser.

Whereas giving directly to a person allows the giver a certain personal proximity with the receiver. This proximity, albeit momentarily, is very much sought by the charity chaser.

The charity chaser heavily profiles their 'opportunities'. They tend to gravitate towards the '*other*', that is, someone who doesn't look like them. They would not want to relate *too* much. There needs to be a psychologically-social barrier. They are likely to profile people from a different race, likely browner than them; someone from a distinctively lower social class, or visible disadvantages like visible disabilities. Their perspective is so biased that when they see the 'others', they would assume poverty and neediness. They often offer their trash even when there is no indication of said neediness. Well, to the charity chaser, the indication would be the profile.

With the proximity and the profiling combined, there is an inevitable power dynamic that is created between all parties involved, to the detriment of the one on the receiving end.

Flashback...

Back in 2015-2016, in the first year of my elder child's life, my family was going through a rough patch. During the first trimester of that pregnancy, I had lost my job as a cultural diversity trainer for a non-profit. My geologist of a husband, being a casualty of the mining crisis in Australia, decided to go back to school to achieve an MBA for professional reconversion. This was the second wave of double unemployment my household experienced, while we had not yet fully recovered from the first wave. We thus ended up with our first child and no income. And you know what they say? When it rains, it pours... A series of incidents added financial strains so much we were drowning and once again living under the poverty line, this time, in a first world country, Australia.

Like a typical Millennial, I joined several parenting groups on social media as soon as I learnt about my pregnancy. I was drawn to natural and attachment parenting communities, which generally tend to be quite community-focused, while being heavily white and privileged.

When news of my dire financial situation was known, the groups organised various ways to help my family and I. Sure, many of the actions helped my family to stay afloat, especially with food at times when we could not buy before welfare payments would arrive. We also had a fair amount of people drop off old clothes and toys for my child. I was offered many things I didn't ask for, nor need, but I said nothing but thank you.

However, I shortly realised that I had become a charity project for many of these group members. I thought I was making new friends who were sharing things with me while I was in a tough place, but really, they showed no interest in getting to know me. They would drop off their donations or do a bank transfer and call it a day. They would not invite me to their place for playdates like they would the other parents in the group or catch up with me on other days just for the sake of socialising. I was only there to satisfy their charitable needs.

A power imbalance was formed where they would be the generous givers, and me the grateful receiver. They would congratulate each other for the care of "[their] underprivileged members". The issue with this power imbalance is that it clashed with who I was and how I wanted to be in that social space.

I'm a trained and experienced community worker and advocate, a diversity trainer and a Black activist; it is in my instincts to call out bigotry when I see it. These circles of privileged parents were full of microaggressions, oppressive attitudes and language, from transphobia to racism and classism. I was almost the only visible Black mother in these groups for a while; I was hyper visible and by nature, loud.

I did not stay quiet and this is when the charity chasers showed their true colours. It didn't take long for me to be labelled as ungrateful because of how much they helped me; how dare I call out their racism? I no longer was "someone who deserves". Even those few who had a modicum of friendship with me (while taking me on as their charity project) would eventually react violently to me calling them out at some point when there was a need for it. There was a tug of war with the charity chasers and other charitable members on one side expecting eternal gratitude and position of power, and myself reclaiming my power, dignity and integrity on the other side.

This was my experience though. I know of many other charity receivers, who unlike me, do not have the confidence, language, and strength to stand up for themselves and rebalance the power dynamic. They end up and remain in this toxic position of being patronised, othered and objectified. *They* are the preferred ones who 'deserve'.

Take note.

If you are a charity chaser, you may be wondering - I hope - on how to unpack your charity-chaserism, because deep down maybe you want to do good. This can surely be achieved by unpacking various aspects that are involved in this process; in the next chapters, I go through all of that.

You need to re-evaluate the concept of charity and the place of decluttering in charitable initiatives, understand the agency and dignity of people in need of support, assess your true intentions and what you are really teaching your kids. These are all crucial steps that will help you shift from being a charity chaser to being a decent human being.

3 DISGUISED RECYCLING

-        Someone who did not mean it in the charity sense.

So wrong!

Spring cleaning comes right in time for charity chasers to prepare their charity boxes. If your definition of gifting others, especially disadvantaged people, is to give old things you no longer use or want, then you are just using them as trash bins. The act of passing a used item to someone else is not the issue. The belief that the only charitable gifts one can make is decluttered items, is.

Commonly, some people drop their donation bags on the receiver's doorsteps, telling them to take what they want and to throw what they don't want away. And too often, receivers end up with the donor's clutter to handle, while having to juggle challenges on their own. The level of audacity and arrogance one must have to believe that their literal trash could be a treasure to someone else based on their disadvantages is astonishing! Yes, I dare say literal *trash* because too often, the condition of these items mean they belong in a bin and not in a donation box.

Let us not forget the old and ugly furniture that people assume poorer families must take because it is free. Sure, in some areas, disposing of clutter can be costly. Across Western Australia, some city councils offer 'verge collection' services; this is an opportunity for residents to put rubbish of any size on the curb for the council to collect and dispose of.

In the northern suburbs of Perth, many councils do not offer a verge collection service but one free industrial waste bin each financial year. This means, if residents across the region have large items to dispose of outside the verge collection or waste bin periods, they would have to take their trash to the dump and recycling site for a fee. Now, sometimes the fee is an issue for some, and sometimes they may judge that their old items are still in good condition and should be used by another. Some people are genuinely concerned about the environmental impact of consumerism and want to foster a culture of recycling old furniture.

They are faced with two options: either to list them on Buy Sell Swap and gifting platforms, or to forcibly offer it to a profiled target. The latter is a dick move that I have too often been subjected to.

Flashback…

When I was a kid at the '*lacaz enba la rivier*', I received quite a lot of donated clothes and toys during Christmas. Very often the clothes had holes, were torn, stained and dirty. Most had missing buttons and broken zips; maybe the donors thought that my mother could "easily fix that". So, then it would mean my mother would buy materials and find time to fix the clothes she didn't ask for.

My mother never fixed these clothes. She used some as rags for cleaning and threw others away. She had so much pride and class despite her social status; she would not allow me to put on clothes that were "*delabre*" (in bad conditions). "Being poor does not mean not having class", she would say.

The toys were often mouldy. The musical items would not play, the dolls almost bald, and often missing an eye. They were preloved items, alright. They were loved until they were unlovable, yet good enough to go to us poor kids. Oh, I remember the playing card packs I got once; I loved playing cards and still do! Only thing is, the pack was not complete. It made sense why the original owners did not want them anymore since they could not play with it, yet it was donated.

My mother would throw away any dirty and broken toys. Maybe the donors also told themselves that we would find our treasure in their trash and throw the rest away? The thing is, '*lacaz enba la rivier*' was not serviced by the council for garbage collection. We had to dispose of our own waste, and the way we did it was not in the environment's best interest; we would burn our trash. There had been a few incidents where the fire went out of control since we lived by the river within a bushy area. Living with danger was our norm anyway.

Years later, when I was a new mother living in poverty in Australia and receiving donation bags from charity chasers, I had my fair share of disgust. Some clothes that were donated had dried food on them, and even vomit. There were stains and urine smells on some of the baby items. I was truly offended and felt quite humiliated. I thought that these 'donors' had no acknowledgement of my universal and inalienable dignity. Even when I was financially challenged, I would never think of giving anyone something that was not in a state for me to use, let alone something they did not ask for.

I remember my Facebook inbox being bombarded with furniture photos from people who had previously donated clothes to me, insisting I take their old furniture. They would even offer to drop it off whilst crossing the emotional manipulation line with their "it is still good and I will have to throw it at the dump site if you don't want it". They made it *my* responsibility to save *their* unbroken item from being destroyed. Refusing was awfully hard when I was still battling with resetting the power dynamic. I was placed in a vulnerable position again in the name of charity.

I am not against hand-me-downs. When I was a kid, we passed on clothes among cousins. As an adult, my friends know that I love fashion, so I often get offered clothes of my taste that they have grown out of or that are not bringing them happiness any longer, thanks to Marie Kondo!

My children, from birth, have been dressed in hand-me-downs mainly from close friends and family members because this is what relatives do; we "network", as my friend Jocelyne puts it. When I recently moved to France, Jocelyne began sending my kids clothes from Norway. Her kids are older than mine and of African descent, so they have cultural as well as winter outfits that I really need and appreciate. In the name of love and friendship, exchanges of old clothes and gifts are regularly made between France and

Norway. Based on such a firm and equal connection, this has nothing to do with charity.

Even when it comes to furniture, I have no problems with second hand items. I would often network furniture with my local friends. In fact, during financially challenging phases, my husband and I would drive around suburbs that were having verge collections. We would take pieces of furniture that we liked and needed for our patio or garden. Someone's trash *was* our treasure, but only when we chose.

Take note.

There are ways to be better humans and manage our own clutter more respectfully and engage in charity. If it is not something in a condition and aesthetics that you would gift yourself, then bin it. Yes, the environment will suffer. It has been made and bought; it has already sealed the environment's fate. You may find some reassurance if the item can be recycled, so make sure you bin it accordingly.

If the items are in good condition and have aesthetics that you would gladly gift yourself, then I ask that you consider the following:

List them up on *Buy Sell Swap* pages to either gain some money or exchange for something else that would be useful for you. If you insist that you want to help disadvantaged people, then go further in your effort to really try to sell those items and donate the money to an established charity or a Christmas appeal that runs during the holiday period. That way, you have dealt with these items you no longer use and have helped someone in a way that they have chosen to receive help.

There are pages for **exchange** where people can list things for free. Use that and allow people to reach out to you for your trash if they have found their treasure. In this way, you respect people's agency. Sure, you will not know the person's socio-economic status and judge whether they are "someone who deserve". But you do not have to know.

Yes, sometimes there are **Christmas appeals** for specific people with specific requests (kids' clothes, furniture, white goods); this is your moment if you don't want to list them for sale. Make sure you stick to what is being asked for. If it is clothes for kids of a certain gender (yes clothes don't have genders but they are sadly heavily gendered) and age, make sure you do not just donate any old kid's clothes to get rid of your clutter. Do not assume they will need more than what has been asked for; Christmas appeals are not opportunities to dump your clutter but are there to satisfy a wish/need list, whether from the shops or your house.

Drop your items at **charity shops**. Yes, customers at op-shops deserve them. Well, to be honest, why would you even think someone *deserves* your unwanted things? What is so special about things you have possessed that the next person needs to *deserve* them? There is a level of arrogance in this mindset and you may want to check that out and come back down to earth, with us. Your old items have no entitlement to any home. If someone chooses to give them a new life, then your old items should be grateful to that person. By "your old item" I mean you, yes.

People of all social classes have agency, and we should not dismiss that because we can sometimes be in a more privileged position. Op-shops are respectful, equal-field options. Coupled with that, many op-shops (at least in Australia and France) employ people who are often discriminated against when it comes to recruitment because of disability, race and language barriers. It should comfort you that with this option, you are indeed helping various people, including yourself.

Something else to understand when it comes to the problematic use of decluttering as an opportunity for charity is that poor people deserve new things too. Poor people deserve new clothes. Poor children should have new clothes for Christmas and New Year. Poor families deserve furniture and appliances in full working condition.

If your response to that is environmental concern, then you should focus on privileged people buying shit daily that actually affects the environment rather than justifying poor people only getting rags. Having new items once a year will never be equal to the damage the rich inflict on the planet. If your own children are not only getting old clothes and old toys wrapped for Christmas, then why would you think donating old clothes to a child will make their Christmas special?

Using the money you made selling your clutter, you could buy new clothes for a child from a Christmas appeal. Using your network, you could organise collectively to fundraise by selling all your clutter to buy one appliance specifically requested in a Christmas appeal. Think of the recipients not as poor people but as...you. What would really make your eye twinkle for Christmas? And most importantly, let them choose.

4 BEGGARS SHOULD BE CHOOSERS

"Beggars can't be choosers".

Well, yes, they can! And they should.

So wrong!

Society expects poorer people to just accept anything they are offered and be grateful for it. Some people really think that a child from a disadvantaged background would be happy receiving any gift for Christmas; this kid should apparently feel the magic of the holiday with the donated old stuffed animal even if they are not into plush toys. Or even, donors would make it a point to focus on what "the child needs". Wants are supposedly only for privileged kids, while privileged adults assume that they know best what poor kids need.

As if poor people are somehow below the basic human characteristics of having tastes, preference and (dietary, ideology and religious) restrictions. How many times do we hear people say that they do not give cash to beggars on the basis that the latter would not spend the money wisely or healthily? Stigmatising poor people as having bad budgeting skills or addiction problems - which in themselves are not shame worthy - are some of the most common misperceptions about poverty. Imbued with these prejudices, privileged people prefer to patronise beggars and eschew the gift of cash in favour of things that were not asked for.

Something quite common that mendicants get instead of cash is food. Each of us have heard at least once of someone saying how they offered a sandwich to a homeless person who - to the interlocutor's dismay - turned down the offering. How many Facebook rants have we read about these alleged "ungrateful" people? A beggar refusing a donation is quite the insult to a charity chaser.

Have these charitable souls ever wondered if the person they are offering food to has any allergy, abstentions or simply do not trust the food presented to them? I do not blame anyone on the streets who refuses food as they are often seen and treated as pests; it is not implausible that the food be poisoned. Homeless people are known to be vulnerable to violence and their cautiousness is understandable.

Even for Christmas appeals, I have noticed that people openly criticise if anything fancy is being requested. Two years ago, I was active in my local community group and there was an appeal for some phones for teenage children of a newly arrived refugee family. The drama this request caused was embarrassing.

"Why do they need a smartphone? A simple phone just to call and text should suffice!"

"Phones are not necessities!"

"I would rather give them food. Where can I drop off?"

The constant policing of poorer people for needing or wanting things that privileged people take for granted is a form of abuse. It is about shaming poor people for expecting more than just basic nourishment, shelter and clothing. It is about making them believe any other 'needs' are just 'wants' that they should not have unless they can afford it themselves. And by affording, they do not mean welfare money; oh no, welfare recipients are not allowed to have anything more than the basics mentioned above or they will be shamed for it!

When it comes to basics, I really mean basic; it is any edible food that they would come across, it is any place they can sleep in, it is any clothing dumped on them by charity chasers. They absolutely must not feel any other way but gratitude for the basics received, let alone aspire to the agency of choice or quality.

Unfortunately, society dehumanises and strips poor people of their legitimate feelings regarding charity offered to them. Standing up for themselves, daring to make their choice known or even refusing, risk them of being labelled as angry, aggressive, or even, fakers. Is one really that poor if they refuse a donation?

Flashback…

December 2010 to March 2011, I was a resident of a Salvation Army women's shelter in Perth, Australia. I was homeless following my escape from a domestic violence (DV) relationship, and the police found me this place mainly dedicated for mothers and children escaping DV. I was childless but the centre made an exception for me.

It was an incredibly challenging time in my life. I was 21 years young, a year and a half since I arrived in this new country as an international student. My family was far away, I felt alone and lost in this big new foreign world. The cycle of abuse theory proved itself to be correct; coming from a childhood of abuse, I ended up in an abusive relationship myself. After 11 months of hell, I was now in a safe place, with various kinds of relevant support. But I felt so much shame for reaching such a low in my life. How did a bright student like me, with aspiration, potential and resolve end up in this situation?

It was not so much about the abuse since I was conditioned to accept being mistreated as the norm. But it was the vulnerability of having no place to call home, whether it was safe or not; the vulnerability of completely relying on charity to survive. I did not have a choice on where I was sleeping.

To be fair, the centre was very well accommodated, and I appreciated my room with my own sanitary facilities; something that many homeless people don't have. I did not have a choice of what I ate. I had what I was given, and many times I could not stomach the food. Sure, they kept me alive and for some not in my shoes, that was all that mattered.

I remember crying in my room some nights…Oh how I missed curry. I spent 21 years of my life mainly eating rice and curry and suddenly my palate was exposed daily to tastes I was not used to, nor enjoyed. Of course, I ate for survival, but some days I did not eat much; I could not. I did sleep hungry sometimes because the sadness that comes with mourning your independence in choosing your food was greater than the hunger. It is a feeling that you may have a hard time grasping if you have not been in that position. I do not wish it on you.

There were occasions where I could choose. For Christmas actually - the hardest of my life so far - when there were donations pouring into the shelter. You guessed it; the charity chasers were at it! Bags of clothes and boxes of toys kept coming every day for weeks. The refuge workers allowed us to go through this trash to find our treasure. I chose a couple of clothing sets, a handbag, and sunglasses. I was chuffed! I liked this shopping for free; no pressure to take anything, no obligation towards the donor and the associated grateful intimacy.

That Christmas Eve night, we had a lovely dinner of ham and vegetables; we sang songs and watched Christmas movies. There was a good vibe among the residents, and I had gotten attached to the kids. Except, the sadness was palpable. When I got to my room to call it a night, I found that a gift was left on my bed. It was a 70cm tall fluffy brown teddy bear with a red bow around it. I hugged it and cried the night away. Kirikou - this is what I named him - became my forever comforter. This Christmas we are going to celebrate our ten years together.

A more recent, and recurrent, memory is about stressful grocery shopping trips. There have been too many occasions in the last five years when my husband and I - like too many other people - are counting down to the last cents with an actual calculator as we scan the grocery aisles. We have had situations when we only had ten dollars available for ten days until any payment came our way. When shopping, every item we put in the cart was a matter of survival; we had to be smart and efficient. Flour, potatoes, rice, canned tuna, eggs were all our choices for cheap but filling meals. Into our cart would be something non-poor people may judge as unnecessary, a little treat. We would sometimes choose even soft drinks or a nice dessert. Had we not exercised a little choice within our ten dollars of shopping, there would not likely be anything other than basic perishables.

Does one who is in survival mode *really* need a treat? Yes, they do. I did. My family did. When we were stressing about whether there will be food tomorrow, well-intentioned people would often tell us to "stay strong" and "keep [our] heads high." How did we keep strong and motivated to keep fighting? By feeling like we were living even just a little instead of merely surviving. Having a treat of our choosing made this happen.

Survival is not just about the body; it is the mind, the sense of self, the will to live. A can of our favourite soft drink may arouse health concerns for some, but for us - with the need to feel 'normal' and alive - it was a medicine. When my heart was palpitating with the anticipated embarrassment at the checkout because we knew that we would have to leave some items behind, what we were trying to hold onto was not unaffordable frivolities, but rather the last bit of control over our choices.

My family benefited from emergency relief food from charity organisations a few times when we did not even have those ten dollars. We have also, at times, had meal trains organised for us by my friends from our local women's support group. They brought us delicious meals; many cooked our preferred dishes or *asked* us what would make us happy. I had a friend who drove a long way to bring her favourite dish she had asked her mother to cook. She wanted to share with me a piece of her childhood and culture. This did not feel like charity, but just people caring for loved ones. It was an exchange. It was equal.

Take note.

Having the choice is more important than one may think. No one knows us better than ourselves, and that includes poor people. Giving a person the choice in the help they receive is acknowledging their sense of self, their agency and dignity. It will also make sure our help is effective and not inadvertently causing harm.

So how can you maximise and respect a person's input when doing charity?

If you are interested in helping a mendicant or homeless person from the street, **stick to cash**. Do not allow concerns about the spending of your donation compromise the right to the benefit of doubt this person has. Recognise your biases and do not act on them.

Sometimes a mendicant or homeless person may welcome food. So, if you have time, and the budget, ask the person if they prefer cash or would like to go to a nearby food outlet to **choose something** to eat. Yes, let them choose if they are happy for you to buy them food. If you are concerned about a strict budget, let them know the budget you have so they can choose within those limits. Do not make remarks about calories or fat in the food they may choose; you must keep your judgements to yourself. If you know that food triggers you, stick to cash.

If you know of anyone in your network (because poor people are not unknown 'others') that may need a bit of uplift at Christmas (or any time of the year) ask them how you may help. But don't do the generic "let me know if you need anything" that most of us hear, **give suggestions** on how you may help. Say things like:

"I can provide hot meals to relieve you of stresses. Let me know what the favourite dishes in your home are. I can also provide money instead so you can cook your own food if you prefer or use the funds any way you judge is the best."

When giving food, be sensitive with your language and demeanour; do not patronise or infantilise. Talk to the person the way you would talk to your respected neighbour.

If you know of someone who urgently needs something, let's say some warm clothes for winter, but you don't have immediate funds nor time to fundraise to buy a new jumper, you may **consider looking at your wardrobe**. You could say something like:

"I have a few jumpers. I can bring them around for you to choose one that suits if you like. I love them all and am happy to let one go to you, friend."

Of course, do not bring your favourite jumper; the difference between this approach and the charity chaser is that instead of dumping your clutter, you are sharing something that you still consider as valuable to you. It is dignifying.

When you see appeals, **do not ask questions** as to why certain requests are being made. Either you contribute or you do not. You are not entitled to any personal history of the person, nor their reasonings. If the appeal resonates with you positively, be as generous as you can, using the notes you took from this book. If you are uncomfortable with the requests, forget about it; the concerned parties need not know your position. Unless, that is, you get dramatic about it on social media, then you are being a dick. Keep your thoughts to yourself, or at least offline to avoid causing further harm to already-vulnerable people.

If you see, or organise, Christmas appeals for families with children, **ask for wish lists** from the children. All kids deserve to get something they genuinely want that will make this holiday special. Encourage your network to participate in buying the wishes from the list. Remember, poor kids deserve new things too!

If you, your organisation, or group traditionally prepare Christmas hampers to give to families, consider adding a **giftcard** in the basket. Do not hesitate to put little treats instead of only basic perishables.

And **be careful** if you are doing a drive by to distribute gifts to homeless children; ask for their age, explain the different options and let them choose from what you have. It is true that at some point you will be left with limited choice options for the last kids; it is not ideal, but it is better than no choice for any kid at all. Drive-bys are tricky as they should be done respectfully otherwise, they are often a complete shitshow.

5 CHARITY TRIPS

-      Charity advertisers doing their best on social media

So wrong!

Let's keep it real. Visually seeing poor people during charity trips will not make your kids understand poverty nor their privilege. 60 minutes spent on a drive-by or half a day volunteering at a charity Christmas event will not put your kids in these poor children's shoes. The realisation of their circumstances will remain superficial. Even as someone coming from a poor background, the awareness and understanding of my situation came years later and amplified with maturity.

Not that children are incapable of seeing realities; but children and adults alike cannot understand the complexity of socio-economic inequalities by giving away toys and soup. No one can fully understand unless one has experienced it. However, awareness can be meaningfully increased by listening to a multitude of diverse voices, understanding the intersectionality of marginalisation that influences each disadvantaged person's experience, and unpacking our biases. Repeatedly, it comes back to biases.

When people with preconceived ideas about a community meet members of said community without the ideal conditions to challenge these ideas, they are likely to reinforce their prejudices based on their corrupted interpretation of the event. Taking your children on charity trips will likely encourage them to *other* people; they will see "the poor", "the homeless", "the beggars", instead of seeing relatable human beings. They will dissociate themselves from *those* people and develop a superiority or saviourism complex - although one could argue they are the same. Your kids will not look at the people being helped as potential friends; they are likely not to see them again.

Sure, children are by nature kind and compassionate. I would have a different narrative if we are talking about young children from privileged backgrounds meeting with children from underprivileged backgrounds, without the interference of biased adults. That would be neutral ground where kids would truly be kids. They are likely to make friends and want to see each other again.

However, charity trips have compromised that neutrality; the kids already know they are going to meet up with the kids that are...different. The child will notice the difference and have their own interpretation of that difference. The adults' language will have an impact on the child prior to the meeting because kids are influenced by their environment. Sadly, it does not take long for them to be harmfully prejudiced.

With charity trips, charity porn is normalised. One must see to be able to care. One must be exposed to someone else's vulnerability and have as many details as possible to accept that the situation is unjust. One feels entitled to ask private questions as if they are buying information with their donation. One must have personal proximity to justify helping. Should children really see to believe that life is not kind to some of their friends?

Flashback...

When I was at the orphanage, there was a very strange practice. Well, I did not think about it then but only since I started therapy as an adult. Tourists, mainly Europeans, would visit the orphanage while on holiday. Sometimes they were couples, and other times families. Their visit involved donations; as I remember it, often after a tourist visit, there would be toys or some special meal.

But what also happened during those visits was all of us kids would be dressed in our Sunday best, our hair combed nicely, and we would be lined up for the visitors. The latter would walk along the line of children and we would greet each other. They would look at us. Inspect us, it felt like. Some kids were up for adoption and some of the visits were for that purpose. Some children would be fostered temporarily by tourists at their rented accommodation. Oh yes, that was a thing back then at this orphanage and we children would be temporarily fostered by some French family in some fancy hotel. Suspicious practice, if you ask me!

So, as we lined up, the tourists would choose one of us if they came for adoption or temporary fostering, or they would just chat with us - them and their kids. They would not eat with us. They would watch us eat. We were actors of a show - a charity show. It speaks of slaves being showcased for sale.

This memory is very triggering to me considering that Mauritius has a history of slavery. My own ancestors were stolen from the east coast of Africa and sent to Mauritius for slavery by Europeans - first the Portuguese, then the French and finally the British. We all know about the live human markets. We have learnt in story books and movies how children were separated from their fathers and mothers and sold. The image of we children lining up after being washed, inspected, asked to smile for potential buyers is not new.

Sure, the intentions of these two situations - tourists at my orphanage and slavers at the market - were different. But the objectification is the same. Whether we are being viewed for purchase or viewed to satisfy one's charity porn thrills, we were dehumanised and othered. I know this will be a tough one for many of you as I have had a few friends who always visit orphanages when they travel to *third world* countries. The questions that one must ask is: "Do I need to see these kids to donate to the organisation? What do these kids gain by meeting me and my kids?"

Take note.

The orphanage is one example of popular charity trips. Whether you are going local or travelling across borders, it is important to evaluate if these trips are necessary. In some cases, they undeniably are, for example, soup kitchens, gift distribution or activity sessions with people. If trips are not necessary, consider donating to relevant organisations without invading the concerned people's privacy and space. If the trips are essential, you can take these steps to minimise harm:

Reconsider if it is necessary to bring your kids, the fewer people the better. For adults as well, there is no need for too many people to go.

For any reason you cannot go without your children, **be mindful** of the language you use to describe the people you are helping and the action you are doing. For example, if you are volunteering at a soup kitchen, consider saying something like: "We are going to serve food to a few people tonight", instead of "we are going to give food to the poor."

For a drive-by, avoid saying things like "for Christmas we need to do good actions and think of the poor. So, let's go give homeless children some gifts." Instead, formulate something like "we want to make sure every child gets a present for Christmas. Someone else will distribute your present another day, so we are distributing other children's presents today."

If you are dropping off, **make it brief**. I guarantee you, donation receivers do not like being overwhelmed and stared at by donors. Of course, poor people are not monolithic; you will have some people who are chatters! You go with the flow. Do not force yourself to talk if you wouldn't normally chat with your respected neighbour. You have your personality too so just be you, while planning for a quick drop off. If during that trip, someone you are donating to wants to chat and you like chatting too, then go for it.

This is not a manual on how to talk to people; absolutely no one can provide you with a manual on a diverse group of social beings. Contained here are pointers, as I mentioned before, on how to engage in a more respectful relationship with poorer people when it comes to gifting. I *can* offer you a short manual on what to teach your children though, since this seems to be a main interest for my fellow socially-conscious parents.

6 TEACHING KIDS

"I want my kids to see these poor children so they can appreciate how good mine have it."

…I have no words.

So wrong!

Parents unashamedly claiming that they use charity porn as teaching materials for their kids to celebrate being on the privileged side of inequality must be one of the most cringeworthy narratives there is. This kind of rhetoric is, however, so normalised it is spread pretty much across cultures and language groups. In the three continental regions I have lived, speaking three different languages, parents use poorer people as teaching props in remarkably similar fashion.

Many of you may think it is important to teach your children about appreciating what they have. The obvious way to learn is by observing those who do not have what your children have, you may argue. Let us unpack this.

Imagine poverty is a disease; let's say a type of cancer. You take your child to *visit* patients at the children's hospital cancer ward where they are receiving volunteers and gifts for Christmas. You particularly want your child to *see* a sick child. When yours sees that patient - because a cancer patient is the only way you would view them - your child has learnt something, according to you. Would you ask your child:

"Now that you have seen this cancer patient kid, are you not happy you do not have cancer? Have you learnt how lucky you are to have a healthy body? You should be grateful."

Bizarre, isn't it, this approach? A child who is not having the best time of their life has strangers come to *view* them in order to feel happy and grateful about their life. What is this and who created this seriously fucked up concept? It is arrogant, disrespectful, impertinent and above all, ignorant. And sadly, most of us parents have had that kind of thought at some point on different issues.

There is absolutely no way, in this scenario, the visiting child will have learnt about the diversity and complexity of cancer in that short time. Even if the kids all played together, cancer is a loaded subject such that this kid would not have learnt anything about it except that it has made some kid's life quite miserable. Coupled with this, comparing the two children makes the visiting child distance himself from the *other* child. The parent has failed to teach the former that nobody is safe from getting sick. The child was not taught how diseases and health work and how one day, sadly, he could be that kid and what then?

Of course, no parent wants to project their child into a possible future of sickness. So, I ask again, what are parents really teaching kids with these exposures? Like this hospital trip, educational charity trips should be questioned. Is poverty in its diversity and complexity understood by just seeing a poor person? Are parents encouraging kids to be happy by not being and looking like those they are giving to charitably? If the child ought to be grateful when they realise their privilege, does it mean that it would be a shame if they happen to lose these privileges? It seems that there is a big misunderstanding from the parents' part on who the people receiving their charity are.

Poverty is a social disease. There are various ways poverty is measured and defined but we are going with the simple and common understanding: *a person living in economic survival mode, with limited to no income and limited to no choices with regards to how their needs are met.* This socio-economic state can either be momentary or long lasting.

In the first instance, poverty can be experienced once or occasionally as episodes throughout a person's lifetime; the result of family, health or economic crisis, or even - perhaps loss of work due to discrimination or industry instability. And anyone is vulnerable to falling victim of losing their financial privileges and slipping under the poverty line. In many cases, some stability is gained after the hard times.

The second instance is systemic; living in generational poverty, and/or attached to a person's identity and social class. This category of poor people may experience less financially challenging phases but the path to reaching a life of financial stability has more obstacles. This mostly concerns communities with descendants of people who suffered ethnic violence and disfranchisement (slavery, genocide, colonisation), people in war-torn regions, people from working class backgrounds who live on the margins of their society or families with disabilities and mental illnesses.

Now, when privileged parents are exposing their children to less privileged children, they are not explaining that people fall victim of socio-economic disparity for various reasons, and in different ways. These kids are not being taught that some of the people they are doing charity for were, once, one of them, and that their privilege today does not protect them from needing help tomorrow. The nuanced relationship that poverty has with race, class, mental health or disabilities will not be explained. The child will not have even been taught the basics about poverty, but rather shown "poor people" as a monolith. Therefore, no, poverty is not being taught in its diversity and complexity.

What the privileged parents are also showing to their kids is poor people as gloomy, uninspiring, and sad. But people living in poverty are more than this state of victimhood. They can be happy in many ways and inspiring and giving… Some are employed *and* homeless. Some are activists and social educators *but* struggle to feed themselves. Some are amazing, supportive, and full of life but counting cents at each grocery shop. Some are artists, some are teachers, some are the friends always available for others to confide in. Poor people are whole, multifaceted, people. Privileged children, if they get to know each of the people they meet on their charity trips, may wish to be more like them and have what they have: the talent, the will, the passion.

Flashback...

My primary school was under a government scheme called *Zone Education Prioritaire*, or *ZEP* (Priority Education Zone). It was a programme that categorised schools in low socio-economic neighbourhoods with a high cohort of underprivileged students. Kids in *ZEP* schools were given daily bread and cheese, milk and semestrial stationery to help improve the learning experience. Our schools would not be the first choice for aspiring and experienced teachers; training, substitute or teachers rejected from elsewhere were who we would normally get.

At the end of six years of primary education, there is a national standardised exam for all school leavers across Mauritius, the Certificate of Primary Education (CPE). At that time, there was a ranking system where the top 2000 ranking students would be listed. For my school-leaving year, there were 60,000 students nationwide for this exam. I gave my ZEP school their first ranking in history.

While I lived with danger in the '*lacaz enba la rivier*' and was surviving child abuse at home, I was also a talented student. I loved reading, had a curious scientific mind, and was quite politically interested from a young age. My family may not have had cable, but I watched every news report and documentary broadcast on the free channels.

My teachers loved me and encouraged me. They helped me register for any academic competition there was for my age, from spelling bees, to writing essays and science projects. I was always representing my school. I bet the other kids I met during these inter-school competitions had no idea of the poverty I was living in. I certainly did not fulfil the stereotypes, instead presenting as smart, enthusiastic, and quite the sunshine as some would describe my big smile.

My mother put a lot on emphasis on education as for her, it was our way out. I knew I had potential, so I dared to dream big. I wanted to become Prime Minister, which changed to becoming Chairperson of the United Nations. Later, I decided I wanted to be a gynaecologist, but then settled on aspiring towards being a pilot. Fortunately, my younger self couldn't foresee a future with obstacles so big that my aspirations would remain as that, aspirations. Little Christelle was unaware that the system was not built for poor little Black girls to have their dreams come true through traditional 'study - succeed' path, and that it has nothing to do with her potential and will. Oh, that blissful ignorance that kept my fire alight...

With my CPE ranking, I got a year scholarship from the city council's Port Louis municipality, recognition in local newspapers, and a place in an elite Catholic high school through an affirmative action programme. I was 12 years old, and my stepfather had inherited his parents' house following their passing. It was the first time I lived in a concrete house, with sanitation. My mother put all her savings into building her beauty salon on the rooftop of our new house. During my first years of high school, I was still way poorer than my classmates and I felt it. I was one of the only kids who did not purchase the expensive school brand bags, jumpers, and coats. I could not afford a lot of the outings. I could not keep up with the demographic of my school and the elitism the school wanted to maintain.

However, I was ranking first in class in many subjects, still getting the attention and interests of teachers, winning academic competitions, and being referred to as a model student.

Imagine me going to a charity Christmas event in my neighbourhood, meeting volunteers with their children. Imagine the latter being told to look at me and be grateful they were not like me. And by like me, I mean the poor they were seeing, not the whole of me which they could not begin to imagine. Would that really have taught a valuable lesson to their child?

Take note.

Teaching values to children is a core parental role. It is natural that parents want to teach their children about humility, gratitude, and generosity – values that I feel are what many parents try to go for when they engage their kids in charity actions. It can all be done, especially during Christmas time, without objectifying poorer people.

One effective and respectful approach would be to explore with children the happiness it brings them when they receive gifts from others. Therefore, we associate receiving gifts with gaining happiness, hence the act of giving as giving happiness (rather than catering to 'need'). We explain to the younger folks that if we are receiving gifts from people, we should be giving to others to make it fair. That is it. You do not have to present yourself as the better positioned, the one with money going to save the poor's Christmas. You remain on the same level of everyone, simply keeping the circle of happiness going.

You can introduce the topic of injustices, including poverty, to your children. No age is too early. Be mindful of your language and your facts. For that you should have unpacked your own biases, again, to better understand the topic at hand. You cannot know everything; do not try to teach what you do not know. If you are socially conscious, you will naturally try to learn about various issues because you care and you want your children to contribute to make the world a better place; this is why we are having this conversation. I see you.

If it is a topic that you do not know much about, like poverty for example, then you could teach your children each time you learn something new. Make sure to translate any information to an age appropriate level. However, I would be cautious of not overwhelming or force-feeding younger people with information. It would be most effective and genuine if you teach them about important topics gradually and organically at the rhythm of their curiosity, and as opportunities arise.

Some more complex understanding comes with maturity, so children do not have to be taught about them if they haven't shown interest in them. For example, understanding the effect of generational trauma of colonisation on Black communities and their relationship with the economy would be something that I would avoid with a young child - unless asked. I would not advise using any profiling language when attempting to refer to race in any discussion on poverty. You do not want your kid to go to school and assume all their browner or disabled friends are poor. They are too young to understand the nuances.

Instead, I would suggest starting by simply explaining that the world is not kind to everyone and does not treat everyone the same. Some people have advantages in some things like being able to go to school and have food every day, but some people have obstacles that hinder those basic rights. There are things we have that others do not have, and there are things others have that we do not have. In order for everyone to be happy, everyone should be able to enjoy everything in life. We should do things to make life enjoyable for everyone. Some other people have been working hard for us to enjoy what we have at home, so we will work to help others enjoy things too. Answer honestly, and simply, any questions that may follow.

This kind of tone and discourse gives a brief description of levels of privileges and disadvantages. It does not *other* the underprivileged people nor place the parent and child in a superior position. It does not require a live show to be understood. Children are smart and are born with compassion. You can guide them to being in tune with their compassion, while minimising the biases that would influence their relationship with society. Before you know it, your children will be doing their own acts of kindness.

7 PARENTAL PRIDE VS THEATRICAL SAVIOURISM

"If I am proud of my kids or something they are doing or I'm teaching, I do post about it but not in a braggy "I am better than you" […] way."

-        a dear friend, engaging in this conversation on Facebook. Used with permission.

Right and wrong!

Of course, we as parents feel pride when our children are making compassionate choices and showing the results of our teachings. And we should let them know that they are seen. It is only natural that when we are amongst our peers, sharing our everyday life, our journey as parents, our parental pride will come out. Showing off the good in their children is how many parents show their love. I get it and it's not my place to dissuade parents from praising their kids even if some people may not favour that idea.

I look at myself as a mother of two, with one child – A - in kindergarten who is starting to show awareness of his surroundings and react compassionately to others. Imagine a hypothetical scenario; A and I are at the playground, I am giving snacks to him, and A offers some of the food to children nearby. He is a social butterfly, makes friends everywhere and is always chatting. It is natural for him to share food with others, just like it is for him to go ask other parents handing out food to their kids for his own share!

But the thing is, I can picture the moment when A will share his food at that playground with a child who possibly does not have any, I will feel much pride. I will certainly share this story with his grandparents and aunties, and uncles, godparents - people who dedicate their lives to following the journey of our children and who guide and inspire them. I am unsure that I would make a Facebook post about it because of my whole "when helping the poor […] don't bring it online" ethic. You know my position on advertised charity.

Let us say that I do brag about A's good action online. There is a big difference between saying:

"I am so proud of A for demonstrating compassion and being selfless with his friends".

As compared to:

"A is so good, he helps poor people when he sees them. He shared his food with this poor fellow who looked like he did not eat the whole day. Our educational charity trips have paid off!"

The first is to me parental pride being respectfully shared in a social setting. The second is nothing but saviourism in all its splendour. With a saviour complex, the parent uses the child who was given the food as the comparison point; privileged child on one side, poor child on the other.

It thus reinforces the *othering* of this kid and places the child that is sharing on pedestal. Instead of focusing on the values the child is demonstrating, the parent is focusing on his position on the socio-economic scale. It is almost like the inherent possession of privilege is being glorified in the name of its ability to help those who lack it.

The privileged person is believed to have saved their underprivileged counterpart. Furthermore, the scenario above suggested that the kid was in fact poor and needed the food. When in reality, my compassionate child sharing food with them is a sweet but basic fact. My interpretation of supposed need services my desire to brag about it in a saviour fashion. This is because the saviour complex encourages us to believe there was a need and we have addressed it.

Saviourism causes harm because the act of doing good comes from a place of preconceptions, privilege, and a comfortable sense of superiority. Sadly, Christmas is the season that puts many underprivileged people at risk of being targeted by *saviours*, often the same charity chasers mentioned before. Saviourism is more prominent though and goes beyond your typical charity chaser; it may concern anyone who is able to help someone else, whether they actively seek charity opportunities or just had the opportunity presented to them. This complex gives the holder a false sense of heroism towards a person that often may not have necessarily needed, nor asked, for that help.

The strong attachment to the idea of *saving* the other person is often attached to feelings of guilt that the saviour is yet to address. The charitable action becomes very personal and emotional for the saviour, and hence is tricked into believing that their action is unchallengeable. After all, they genuinely want to do good!

Flashback...

In 2016, Philando Castile and Alton Sterling - two Black American men - were killed by police. The murders were caught on camera and the footage widely shared on social media. There followed a series of Black Lives Matter protests across America, Europe, and Australia.

Alongside a group of activists in Perth, I co-organised a protest as a response to police brutality against Black bodies in America and Australia. There were about six of us main organisers who had been defending some causes and advocating for marginalised communities in our part of the world. Two people on the team were university lecturers, some were students, and I was a community worker and advocate who was about to go back to Law school for further studies. All of us were People of Colour.

During the organisation process, a middle-aged white lady - Ms L - reached out to us to offer her help. Of course, we knew that we would need various kinds of help, so we welcomed anyone committed to help get things moving; we had a team of volunteers ready to be assigned roles and have tasks delegated. Ms L would regularly be contacting and questioning the youngest member of our team to get updates on our progress. This is how she learnt of our upcoming meeting with the police that was required to get authorisation for our plans, establish our limits and assess the risks involved. When the team arrived for our meeting with the Chief police officer of Perth Police, we were shocked to find Ms L had arrived without informing us. Not only that, but she had also turned up earlier than scheduled to start the conversation with the police. The rest of us *joined* in like mere assistants.

Ms L took over the conversation completely and the police barely even exchanged a word with us - the three main organisers. For professionalism's sake, we did not interrupt her during the meeting. The police had asked that we designate a person from our team to be liaising with them on the day of the event. After the meeting, we questioned Ms L as to why she had come without informing us prior, and why she had started the conversation without us. Her answer was as honest as she could be:

"I knew the police would not take a group of young Black people seriously, so I came as I knew how to talk to them, and they can trust me."

This is what saviourism looks like. She was so proud of herself. We were upset. She was confused as to why we were upset. She kept reminding us that she had taken time out of her day to *help* us, how she did not mind spending money on "expensive parking tickets in the middle of the city" as it was important "for the cause". But no one asked her for that, and yet she was praising herself based on what she *thought* we needed help with.

The organising team discussed the incident later in private and decided that Ms L should take a step back and let us keep doing what we do well: organise a rally. Many of us had done this many times, but she had assumed that because of our race, we would not know how to handle a police meeting. Sure, discrimination exists, and this protest was just about that. But her assumption that she needed to use her privilege to save us from an oppression she benefited from, and would continue to reap, only reinforced this system of oppression. Her behaviour upheld the stereotypes she claimed to fight against. In essence, she was pretty much saying, "it is how it is, so let my white self protect you".

Our team contained members of all genders. We decided to allocate the role of Police Liaison Officer to a Queer Woman of Colour who would know how to defend our interests if need be. It was also an empowering role, given the context. We communicated her information to the police and informed

Ms L of our decision; she had been bombarding us with emails and texts about 'her' role. She even planned to make a speech at the protest. We refused. This is when it started to get ugly. Ms L contacted various people to say how she was being discriminated against by our team because of her race. She would list all the various places she had "helped people". Seeking to prove her charitable heart, she would send us photos of her at protests for Aboriginal people or for the environment. She would tell us how ungrateful we were after all she had done for the cause. She wanted a role for validation.

And this is what it boils down to when it comes to a saviour complex: validation. They need to be loud and seen. It centres on that need to make it all about heroism. Being in the shadows or discretion is not an option. Little did Ms L know that among the six of us main organisers, three who were non-Black People of Colour decided not to make a speech rather than take space from Black voices. They knew they didn't need to be seen in order to do their part. Something someone with a saviour complex does not understand.

Take note.

If you want to praise your kids for a charitable act they have done, consider your audience and ask yourself why you are doing this. Is it to validate your child? You could perhaps let them know directly that you are proud of them for their actions. By posting it online and making a show of it, or letting it be known to a group of people you meet, how is that validation to your child? Could it be that the validation sought is mostly for you?

When I think of it, I can see myself doing that with the extended family; I am guilty too of seeking validation as a mother, to be recognised as succeeding in my role. We all do this as we are all humanly imperfect. However, we must be honest with ourselves and recognise that what we are doing is unnecessary and comes from underlying issues with ourselves.

I want to take it further and even question *how* we praise our kids after they helped someone. I would suggest congratulating your child for being in touch with their compassionate nature and caring for others, reminding them of how others care for them too.

If you make a big deal out of them doing the minimum a decent human being should and congratulate them each time for it, then you are not normalising that action. You might even be fostering a saviour complex within them, which is the opposite of what you want to do. Make sharing become the norm. It is not hard at all. It may all look very complex, but if you sit down, question everything you do, the charity boxes, the trips, the language you use with kids and how you talk about Christmas and charity to your friends, all will slowly make sense.

Above all, you need to be sure of your intentions.

8 INTENTIONS

"Why am I really doing this?"

This is the question you need to ask yourself each time you feel like helping someone on charitable grounds.

So wrong!

I trust that you now know all the different reasons why you should not think of doing charity, especially this Christmas.

- You have done your spring cleaning and need to rid yourself of all these boxes of clothes and other pre-loved items.

- You need proof that you are a good person.

- You want to save Christmas for poor children.

- You want your kids to embrace their position of privilege.

- You want to teach your kids.

- Or you want to soothe yourself from the guilt you feel about having privilege.

If, when you question your own intentions before you do a donation and the answer is one of the above, stop. Reflect. Read this book again. Re-evaluate why you should be doing charity.

Be right!

No, I am *not* saying do not give at all. Well, I gave you multiple examples on how to give respectfully and efficiently. I believe you can shift your intentions from one of the above to more dignified reasons.

Do it for the *person* and no one else

If someone needs help or cheering up, do it for them and them only. Do not do it thinking about what you or your children will gain from it. Do not even do it so that you get rewarded divinely according to your spiritual or religious belief. Be selfless. This approach will help you centre the needs of the person you want to help. Consequently, you will less likely cause unintentional harm but instead develop trust with that person. This is important as many people who do need help hesitate to ask for it because they do not want to be pawns, nor be disrespected in the process. The person receiving charity from you needs to feel you are not in it for something, and that they are safe to accept your donation.

Favour *discretion*

Give and make peace with the fact that no one may know about it. Yes, it also applies to your children so they can model that important skill from you. It is a skill for sure to be able to do something that has impacted on someone's Christmas, for example, and letting go of any kind of recognition. It is the only logical path for giving selflessly though, isn't it?

Even with the person that you have donated to, you should try and not bring that up unless the person in question initiates the conversation. If you find opportunities to remind a person you have helped, they might question your intentions. People who receive charity are often quite uncomfortable to see and talk to their donors, especially if the power dynamic is significantly affected. Again, trust needs to be built and the person needs to feel safe with you and not feel as if they owe you. Surely it is not your intention to give and make the person feel bad? So, let go of the need to talk about your donation. It is done and gone.

Not to use your privilege but to *decrease*, or eliminate the margins

Do not get attached to the idea of you being in a position of privilege and that you will help because you *can*. In my opinion, this only reinforces the status quo of you being on one favourable side and the *other* being on the unfavourable side. Help because everybody deserves to eat, everybody deserves to have a good time, every child deserves a magical Christmas. You want to disrupt the system that leaves people in unacceptable conditions. Sure, a donation will not eliminate the margins by eradicating classism and poverty. This fight is multi-layered, and must be taken by different bodies, from various sides, both structural and personal. But one good angle of attack on this injustice is to willingly want things to be fair for the underprivileged people.

For example, you might go about life as usual and give a donation - an amount or a gesture that is insignificant to your own comfort - and you'll tell yourself you have used your position of privilege to do good. This approach will not have any positive impact on the bigger picture. Instead, if you think it is unfair that your children will have a good Christmas but other children around you may not, and you become uncomfortable with that idea, you might want to do something more impactful. You are likely to put that person's needs first, and your actions or donations are likely to significantly influence the journey of this person.

This proactive approach means you are likely to engage in the fight against the -isms responsible for those socio-economic disparities. Perhaps you will rethink your own role in the system and your personal contribution to the inequalities. You will put meaning into charity and your kids will witness all of that and learn about the important values you hold dear.

Shifting from "charity" to "*sharing*"

This includes shifting the associated thinking about "charity" as we know it to "sharing". The acts might be the same but the emotional connection we have with acts will change as well. It will help us connect to the other, put ourselves on the same level, feel like a community instead of an outsider coming in to donate and then leave.

When we share, we give a bit of what we have, we give our good intentions, and we give our genuineness. Also, if we think about charity as sharing, we acknowledge that we also receive from other people. Coupled with that, while sharing selflessly with no expectation, you will organically receive many things in return; whether it is inspiration, a chance to introspect, a friendship, smiles, the laughter of children, ultimately you will come out of it with something that will improve and deepen your life.

Flashback…

It was in 2017 that my family hit the lowest point. The crash in the iron ore industry in Australia is what instigated my husband's attempted career change by studying for an MBA. I was a full-time student in Law school, while we were also caring for A who was a toddler. We had no income apart from welfare payments; contrary to classist beliefs, a family cannot sustain on welfare assistance only. We were destitute. At that time, we were living off emergency relief food, our bank accounts were always in the red, and grocery trips came with a risk of being humiliated with a card payment being declined. My husband was the one doing the grocery shopping.

He was badly hit. I guess, I had the tools to survive poverty and learn to live and find happiness at the same time. My husband was merely surviving. He was born and grew up in a wholly different world to mine. His educational path was conventional. He got a high paying job in Australia. He did not anticipate poverty.

The first wave of the crisis was in 2013. Then it was up and down. We had our tough times in 2015, but then after he graduated from his MBA with Distinction, we had hoped the tide would change for us. He had been waiting for the moment when his talent and hard work would support his family and allow him to give us comfort and stability. It did not happen. Anyone can sympathise with a husband and father's disappointment and the subsequent shame at not being able to provide for his family in the way he wanted and was capable of. His mental health plummeted. He had reached breaking point…

Out of concern and desperation, I reached out to his family in France to inform them of his mental state. Understanding the urgency to intervene, they offered to pay for his and A's flight tickets to France, while my friend paid mine. This trip was to help him reconnect with himself, refill his cup with the love and support of his extended family. He is very much a family man. They are his anchor. We all are. Within three weeks of me contacting his family, we were in France.

Whilst in France, we started debating the possibility of moving our family there in order to benefit from the support and protection of his extended family. I visited universities. I tried to imagine myself relocating to France, but it was very hard. Australia had become my home, and despite the financial struggles, I loved my life there. Being poor did not phase me because I had an active, productive, life regardless. I *was* attracted to the promise of unconditional support though. But I needed to confide in my friends and sort out my own thoughts.

One of my friends I had been talking to learnt about how bad the financial situation was for me in Australia. She listened to me vent and cry. She validated my feelings. She helped me weigh the pros and cons of moving to France and she never judged me.

She then asked me for my PayPal address, and transferred $2000 to my account. It was a gift she said. She was in a privileged position. I was shocked. I thanked her. I stayed shocked for a while. She never told me what to do with it. She never asked what I did with it. She never even spoke of it ever again. I know that she has not talked about it with other people in our circle of friends.

Today we are still good friends. We do not talk regularly, but I feel no pressure in regard to her, nor feel that I owe her, which is very different to some other people who have given us much less than that. There have been occasions since when I have called her out on some irrelevant issues, and she has also challenged me on something problematic I said that might have hurt her. We have a healthy relationship, where I do not feel a battle of power. What she did was charitable, but it did not feel like *charity*. It felt that she shared something of hers with me. I felt dignified.

This Christmas, I wish for everyone to experience how my friend was with me and my family and, if you've absorbed the message in this book, you'll understand it's never been about the amount and it needs no advertising. This is the best gift you can give.

51

ABOUT THE AUTHOR

Christelle is a Black Queer activist, emerging writer, spoken word poet and textile artist at Ubuntu Fibres. Born in 1989 in Rodrigues Island, Mauritius, she found her way to Australia as an international student in 2010, where she spent the next decade, and gained citizenship. She writes in Mauritian Creole, French and English.

Building on her success to achieve a place in the top 15% of UWA Law School, Christelle has focused on researching the effect of racial bias on crime rates in Australia. She has worked as a diversity educator and inclusion consultant, advocated for vulnerable communities on executive boards and led initiatives such as Project One Heart - interviewing People of Colour and Queer parents across Australia to share their stories and voices with the world.

Outside of academia, Christelle enjoys memoir writing that recalls moments in her tumultuous life. Her crafted words expose raw honesty that digs into her own vulnerability to highlight aspects about humanity and society that need to be challenged. Whether in her writing, weaving or cloth painting, Christelle harnesses storytelling to help people see, remember and understand. Much of her writing and artistic work can be found at www.UbuntuFibres.com

Christelle currently resides in France